Churros Cookbook 101

Mouthwatering Recipes for Crafting Irresistible Churros and Exploring Creative Variations

CHURROS COOKBOOK 101

First edition. January 17, 2024.

Copyright © 2024 john ahmad.

ISBN: 979-8224526345

Written by john ahmad.

Table of Contents

John Ahmad

Chapter 1: Introduction to Churros

Churros, those delightful fried pastries with their irresistibly crispy exteriors and soft, doughy interiors, have captured the hearts and taste buds of people around the world. In this chapter, we'll delve into the rich history and origin of churros, uncovering the intriguing journey that led to their global popularity.

1. The History and Origin of Churros

Churros' origins can be traced back to Spain, where they are believed to have been inspired by the culinary traditions of the Iberian Peninsula. A fascinating blend of Moorish, Spanish, and Portuguese influences contributed to the creation of this beloved treat.

Ancient Beginnings: The story of churros starts in ancient times, where the Moorish occupation of the Iberian Peninsula introduced the concept of frying dough. The precursor to churros may have been a sweet treat known as "zalabiya," a deep-fried dough soaked in honey.

Spanish Heritage: As Spain emerged from Moorish rule, the churro began to take shape. Spanish shepherds are said to have cooked strips of dough over an open flame, creating a crispy and satisfying snack that resembled the churros we know today.

Churros in the New World: Churros' journey didn't stop in Spain. Spanish explorers brought this culinary delight to the New World, where it took on new forms and flavors. In Mexico, churros were often filled with chocolate or dulce de leche, adding a new layer of indulgence.

2. Why Churros Are Loved Worldwide

The universal appeal of churros lies in their delectable simplicity and versatility. Let's uncover the reasons behind their worldwide popularity.

Texture and Flavor Fusion: Churros are a delightful fusion of textures and flavors. The contrast between the crispy exterior and the soft, doughy interior is nothing short of addictive. This unique combination makes churros perfect for pairing with an array of coatings, toppings, and fillings.

Street Food Sensation: Churros found their way onto the streets of many countries, where they became a beloved street food. The sight and aroma of freshly fried churros being dusted with sugar or dipped in rich chocolate evoke a sense of nostalgia and comfort.

Churros in Modern Cuisine: In the modern culinary landscape, churros have transcended their humble origins. Creative chefs and home cooks alike have embraced churros as a canvas for innovation. From churro ice cream sandwiches to churro-inspired pancakes, the possibilities are endless.

Cultural Significance: Churros have become an integral part of cultural celebrations and gatherings. Whether it's a lively fiesta, a carnival, or a special family occasion, churros have a way of bringing people together and adding a touch of festive joy.

As we journey through the pages of this cookbook, we'll not only learn how to master the art of crafting churros but also gain a deeper understanding of the cultural heritage and global influence that have made these treats a cherished delight. In the next chapter, we'll explore the essential tools and ingredients you'll need to embark on your churro-making adventure.

Chapter 2: Essential Churro-Making Tools and Ingredients

Before you embark on your churro-making journey, it's important to equip yourself with the right tools and gather high-quality ingredients that will help you create the perfect churros every time. In this chapter, we'll explore the essential equipment your kitchen should have and the key ingredients that are crucial for crafting churros that are crispy, flavorful, and simply irresistible.

1. Must-Have Equipment in Your Kitchen

Churro Press or Piping Bag: A churro press or a sturdy piping bag with a star tip is essential for creating the classic ridged shape of churros. It allows you to control the size and shape of the dough as it's piped into the hot oil.

Deep Fryer or Heavy Pot: A deep fryer or a heavy pot is required for frying the churros. Make sure it's deep enough to allow the churros to float freely in the oil without touching the bottom.

Candy Thermometer: A candy thermometer is crucial for maintaining the right frying temperature. Consistent heat is key to achieving that perfect golden-brown crunch.

Slotted Spoon or Spider Strainer: These tools are used to carefully place the churros into the hot oil and to remove them once they're cooked to perfection.

Cooling Rack: A cooling rack is essential for draining excess oil from the fried churros, helping them maintain their crispiness.

Pastry Brush: A pastry brush comes in handy for brushing excess flour off the churros before frying and for applying coatings like cinnamon sugar.

2. Key Ingredients for Perfect Churros

All-Purpose Flour: High-quality all-purpose flour forms the base of churro dough, giving it the structure it needs while allowing for a light and airy texture.

Water: Water is the primary liquid used in churro dough, and its temperature plays a role in achieving the right consistency.

Salt: A small amount of salt enhances the flavor of the dough and balances the sweetness of the coatings.

Sugar: Sugar adds sweetness to the dough and helps create a beautifully golden-brown exterior when fried.

Unsalted Butter: Butter enriches the dough, contributing to its flavor and tenderness.

Eggs: Eggs provide structure and moisture to the dough, resulting in a tender interior.

Vanilla Extract: Vanilla extract adds a delightful aroma and depth of flavor to the churros.

Oil for Frying: Use a neutral oil with a high smoke point, such as vegetable or canola oil, for frying the churros.

Cinnamon and Sugar: This classic coating adds a warm and comforting flavor to churros, making them a beloved treat.

Optional Ingredients: Depending on the type of churros you're making, you may need additional ingredients such as cocoa powder for chocolate churros, fruit preserves for filled churros, or cheese for savory variations.

By understanding the importance of each tool and ingredient, you'll be well-prepared to dive into the churro-making process. Armed with the right equipment and the finest ingredients, you'll be on your way to creating churros that are not only delicious but also a true work of art. In the upcoming chapters, we'll start crafting churros with classic cinnamon sugar coating and explore a variety of delightful variations.

Chapter 3: Basic Churro Dough Recipe

The foundation of every delicious churro lies in the dough itself. In this chapter, we'll dive into the heart of churro-making by providing you with a step-by-step guide to creating the perfect churro dough. From mixing the ingredients to achieving the ideal consistency, we'll walk you through the process so you can master the art of crafting churros that are crispy on the outside and delightfully tender on the inside.

1. Step-by-Step Dough Preparation

Gather Your Ingredients: Assemble all the necessary ingredients for your churro dough, including all-purpose flour, water, salt, sugar, unsalted butter, eggs, and vanilla extract.

Prepare the Dough: In a saucepan, combine water, butter, sugar, and salt. Heat the mixture until the butter melts and the mixture begins to simmer.

Add Flour: Remove the saucepan from heat and quickly stir in the all-purpose flour until the mixture forms a smooth, cohesive dough.

Incorporate Eggs: Beat the eggs in a separate bowl and gradually add them to the dough, mixing well after each addition. The dough should become glossy and slightly sticky.

Add Vanilla Extract: Mix in a splash of vanilla extract to enhance the flavor of the dough.

2. Tips for Achieving the Right Consistency

Balancing Moisture and Flour: Achieving the perfect churro dough consistency is crucial. The dough should be soft and slightly sticky but manageable enough to be piped.

Avoid Overmixing: Once you've added the eggs, avoid overmixing the dough. Overmixing can lead to tough churros. Mix just until the dough is smooth and glossy.

Piping Technique: Load the churro dough into a churro press or a piping bag fitted with a star tip. Hold the bag at a 45-degree angle and pipe the dough directly into the hot oil, using scissors or a knife to cut the dough at your desired length.

Frying Temperature: Maintain the oil temperature at around 350-375°F (175-190°C). Too low of a temperature can result in greasy churros, while too high of a temperature can cause uneven browning.

Test and Adjust: Fry a small piece of dough first to test the oil temperature and ensure the churros cook evenly. Adjust the heat if needed.

Consistency Check: The churro dough should produce churros with a crispy exterior and a light, airy interior. Aim for churros that are golden brown and cooked through.

Mastering the Technique: Churro dough consistency may take a few tries to perfect. Don't be discouraged if your first batch isn't exactly as you envisioned. Practice and experience will help you achieve the desired results.

By following these step-by-step instructions and implementing the tips for achieving the right consistency, you'll be well on your way to creating a flawless basic churro dough. Once you've mastered this foundational recipe, you'll be ready to explore a world of churro variations and experiment with different coatings, fillings, and flavors in the chapters that follow.

Chapter 4: Classic Cinnamon Sugar Churros

The quintessential churro experience wouldn't be complete without the timeless combination of cinnamon and sugar. In this chapter, we'll guide you through the process of achieving perfectly fried churros with a golden, crispy exterior, and show you how to coat them in a heavenly layer of cinnamon sugar. Get ready to indulge in the comforting flavors of these classic treats that have delighted generations.

1. Frying Techniques for Golden Crunchiness

Oil Temperature Mastery: Maintain the oil temperature within the recommended range of 350-375°F (175-190°C). This ensures that the churros fry evenly and develop that desirable crispy texture.

Piping and Frying: Use a churro press or a piping bag to pipe the dough into the hot oil. Make sure not to overcrowd the pan, as this can lower the oil temperature and affect the churros' crunchiness.

Turning and Flipping: As the churros fry, use tongs to gently turn and flip them for even browning. Keep an eye on their color and adjust the frying time accordingly.

Draining Excess Oil: Once the churros are beautifully golden brown, carefully remove them from the oil using a slotted spoon or spider strainer. Allow them to drain on a paper towel-lined plate or cooling rack to remove any excess oil.

2. Coating Churros with Cinnamon Sugar

Prep Your Cinnamon Sugar Mixture: While the churros are still warm, prepare the cinnamon sugar coating. In a bowl, combine granulated sugar and ground cinnamon. The ratio can be adjusted to suit your taste preferences.

Coating the Churros: While the churros are still slightly warm, gently roll them in the cinnamon sugar mixture until they are evenly coated. You can also place the churros in a paper bag with the cinnamon sugar and shake to coat.

Tapping off Excess Coating: Once coated, tap the churros lightly to remove any excess cinnamon sugar. This ensures a balanced flavor without overwhelming sweetness

Serving and Enjoying: Classic cinnamon sugar churros are best enjoyed fresh and warm. Serve them immediately, and watch as the sweet aroma and irresistible crunchiness make them an instant favorite.

Variation: Churro Dipping Sauces: To enhance the experience, consider serving your classic cinnamon sugar churros with a variety of dipping sauces, such as warm chocolate ganache, caramel sauce, or fruit coulis.

By mastering the art of frying churros to golden perfection and expertly coating them with cinnamon sugar, you'll be able to recreate the cherished classic churro experience right in your own kitchen.

Chapter 5: Decadent Chocolate-Dipped Churros

Indulge your senses in the luxurious world of chocolate-dipped churros. In this chapter, we'll guide you through the art of tempering chocolate to create a smooth and glossy coating for your churros. Whether you prefer dark, milk, or white chocolate, we'll show you how to achieve that perfect chocolate dip. Plus, we'll explore creative toppings and drizzles that will take your churros to new heights of decadence.

1. Tempering Chocolate for Coating

Understanding Tempering: Tempering chocolate is a precise process that involves melting and cooling chocolate to specific temperatures. This ensures that the chocolate sets with a shiny finish and a satisfying snap.

Chocolate Selection: Opt for high-quality chocolate bars or chocolate chips with a cocoa content that suits your taste. Dark chocolate (around 70% cocoa), milk chocolate, and white chocolate are popular choices.

Melting Chocolate: Break the chocolate into small, uniform pieces. Melt two-thirds of the chocolate using a double boiler or in the microwave, using short intervals and stirring frequently.

Cooling and Reheating: Pour the melted chocolate onto a cool, clean surface (marble slab or baking sheet) and spread it to cool and thicken. Once it reaches a lower temperature, mix it back into the remaining melted chocolate to bring it to the ideal working temperature.

2. Creative Toppings and Drizzles

Chopped Nuts: After dipping the churros in chocolate, immediately roll them in a mixture of finely chopped nuts, such as almonds, hazelnuts, or pistachios. The nuts adhere to the chocolate, adding a delightful crunch and nutty flavor.

Toffee Bits: Sprinkle small toffee bits over the wet chocolate coating. The toffee will embed itself in the chocolate as it sets, creating a sweet and buttery contrast to the rich chocolate.

Coconut Flakes: Submerge the freshly dipped churros into a bowl of shredded coconut. The coconut adheres to the chocolate, imparting a tropical and textural twist.

Colorful Sprinkles: Decorate your churros with a shower of colorful sprinkles or nonpareils. Coordinate the colors with the type of chocolate you're using for a visually appealing treat.

Fruit Zest: Enhance the flavor of your chocolate-dipped churros by grating citrus zest, such as orange or lemon, directly over the wet chocolate. The zest infuses the chocolate with a refreshing and aromatic essence.

Drizzling Magic: Use a fork or a piping bag to elegantly drizzle contrasting chocolate or caramel sauce over the dipped churros. Let your creativity flow as you create intricate patterns that adorn the churros' surface.

Presentation Perfection: Place your artfully adorned chocolate-dipped churros on a decorative platter. Dust them with a light sprinkling of powdered sugar for an extra touch of elegance.

As you master the delicate art of tempering chocolate and experiment with an array of creative toppings and drizzles, you'll transform your churros into decadent delights that are as visually stunning as they are delectable.

Chapter 6: Fruity Flair: Berry-Filled Churros

Embark on a journey of delightful contrasts with berry-filled churros. In this chapter, we'll explore the art of crafting churros filled with luscious fruit compotes that add a burst of freshness and natural sweetness to every bite. Learn how to prepare tantalizing fruit fillings and master the piping techniques that transform these churros into exquisite treats that are as beautiful as they are delicious.

1. Making Fruit Compotes for Filling

Fruit Selection: Choose a medley of fresh, ripe berries such as strawberries, raspberries, blueberries, or blackberries. These vibrant fruits lend themselves perfectly to creating flavorful compotes.

Preparation: Wash and clean the berries, removing any stems or leaves. Depending on the berries, you can leave them whole or chop them into smaller pieces.

Cooking the Compote: In a saucepan, combine the berries with a touch of sugar and a splash of citrus juice (lemon or orange). Gently cook the mixture until the berries break down and release their juices, creating a thick and flavorful compote.

Straining: Once the compote has cooled slightly, strain it through a fine mesh sieve to remove any seeds or solids. This yields a smooth and velvety filling that's perfect for piping into churros.

2. Piping Techniques for Stuffed Churros

Preparing the Dough: Prepare a batch of churro dough following the basic recipe. For stuffed churros, the dough should be slightly thicker to hold the filling.

Piping Bags and Tips: Use a sturdy piping bag fitted with a star tip. Fill the bag with the churro dough, leaving enough space for the compote filling.

Creating a Hollow Center: Pipe a length of churro dough onto a baking sheet, leaving a space in the middle for the filling. You can achieve this by using your finger to create a well along the length of the dough.

Adding the Filling: Using another piping bag, fill the hollow center with the berry compote. Be generous, as the filling is what gives these churros their fruity flair.

Sealing and Cutting: Pipe another layer of churro dough over the compote filling, sealing it completely. Use scissors or a knife to cut the churros into your desired length.

Frying and Presentation: Fry the stuffed churros following the frying techniques you've learned. As they cool, these berry-filled churros will develop a beautiful two-tone appearance, with the fruit filling peeking through.

Serving Suggestions: Dust the berry-filled churros with powdered sugar and serve them with a drizzle of chocolate sauce or a dollop of whipped cream for a truly decadent experience.

With the knowledge of crafting fruit compotes for filling and mastering the art of piping stuffed churros, you're well on your way to creating a mouthwatering masterpiece that combines the freshness of berries with the satisfying crunch of churros.

Chapter 7: Savory Twists: Cheese-Stuffed Churros

Prepare to tantalize your taste buds with an unexpected twist on churros. In this chapter, we'll dive into the savory world of cheese-stuffed churros, where the combination of rich, gooey cheese and the satisfying crunch of churros creates a flavor explosion like no other. Learn about various types of cheese fillings, discover the art of crafting these savory delights, and explore a variety of delectable dipping sauces that perfectly complement the cheesy goodness.

1. Types of Cheese Fillings

Cheddar and Jalapeño: Combine sharp cheddar cheese with diced jalapeños for a spicy kick that balances the richness of the cheese.

Creamy Brie and Fig: Experience the luxurious pairing of creamy brie cheese with sweet fig preserves, creating a harmonious blend of flavors and textures.

Smoked Gouda and Bacon: Embrace the smoky and savory notes of smoked gouda cheese, enhanced with crumbled bacon for an indulgent treat.

Goat Cheese and Herb: Elevate your cheese-stuffed churros with tangy goat cheese and a medley of fresh herbs, such as chives, thyme, and parsley.

2. Pairing with Dipping Sauces

Savory Tomato Jam: A savory tomato jam adds a burst of tangy-sweet flavor that complements the richness of the cheese-stuffed churros.

Creamy Herb Dip: Create a velvety herb-infused dipping sauce using a blend of sour cream, fresh herbs, garlic, and a squeeze of lemon juice.

Honey Mustard Drizzle: The combination of honey and mustard offers a delightful contrast to the savory cheese filling, adding a touch of sweetness and tang.

Garlic Parmesan Dip: Craft a creamy dip by blending grated parmesan cheese, roasted garlic, and Greek yogurt. This dip enhances the cheesiness of the churros.

Balsamic Reduction: Drizzle a balsamic reduction over your cheese-stuffed churros to add depth and complexity to each bite.

3. Crafting Cheese-Stuffed Churros

Preparing the Dough: Follow the basic churro dough recipe, but adjust the sugar and omit the vanilla extract to create a savory base for the cheese filling.

Filling the Churros: Fill a piping bag with the cheese filling of your choice. Pipe the cheese filling into the center of the churro dough as you pipe it onto a baking sheet.

Sealing and Frying: Ensure the cheese filling is fully enclosed within the dough. Fry the churros using the frying techniques you've mastered, aiming for a beautiful golden-brown hue.

Serving and Enjoying: Pair the cheese-stuffed churros with your preferred dipping sauces and watch as the unexpected savory twist takes your taste buds on a delightful journey.

With the knowledge of crafting various types of cheese fillings and expertly pairing them with dipping sauces, you'll have the skills to create savory cheese-stuffed churros that are sure to impress your guests.

Chapter 8: Exotic Delights: Churros from Around the World

Spanish Churros con Chocolate
Churros Ingredients:

- 1 cup water
- 2 tablespoons unsalted butter
- 2 teaspoons granulated sugar
- ¼ teaspoon salt
- 1 cup all-purpose flour
- 3 large eggs
- Vegetable oil, for frying

Cinnamon Sugar Coating:

- ½ cup granulated sugar
- 1 teaspoon ground cinnamon

Chocolate Dipping Sauce:

- 1 cup dark chocolate chips
- ½ cup heavy cream
- Pinch of salt

Instructions:
For Churros:

1. In a saucepan, combine water, butter, sugar, and salt. Bring to a simmer over medium heat.
2. Remove from heat and add all-purpose flour. Stir

vigorously until the mixture forms a smooth dough.

3. Let the dough cool for a few minutes, then beat in the eggs one at a time until fully incorporated and the dough is glossy.
4. Transfer the dough to a piping bag fitted with a star tip.
5. Heat vegetable oil in a deep fryer or heavy pot to 375°F (190°C).
6. Pipe strips of dough directly into the hot oil, cutting them with scissors or a knife. Fry until golden brown and crispy, about 2-3 minutes per side.
7. Remove churros with a slotted spoon and drain on paper towels.

For Cinnamon Sugar Coating:

1. In a shallow bowl, combine granulated sugar and ground cinnamon.
2. While the churros are still warm, roll them in the cinnamon sugar mixture to coat evenly.

For Chocolate Dipping Sauce:

1. In a small saucepan, heat heavy cream until it just starts to simmer.
2. Remove from heat and add dark chocolate chips and a pinch of salt.
3. Let sit for a minute, then stir until the chocolate is fully melted and the sauce is smooth.

To Serve:

1. Arrange the cinnamon sugar-coated churros on a

serving plate.

2. Serve the churros warm with the homemade chocolate dipping sauce on the side.
3. Dip the churros into the chocolate sauce and enjoy the delightful combination of textures and flavors.

This Spanish Churros con Chocolate recipe will transport you to the streets of Spain, where you can savor the comforting delight of crispy churros dipped in rich chocolate. Feel free to explore more recipes from the cookbook's other chapters for a complete churro-making experience!

Chapter 9: Healthier Alternatives: Baked Churros

Indulge your cravings guilt-free with a healthier twist on the classic churro. In this chapter, we'll explore the world of baked churros, where the oven takes center stage to create crispy, flavorful treats without the need for frying. Discover the benefits of baking versus frying, master the techniques for achieving perfectly crisp baked churros, and uncover the secrets to keeping the taste and texture intact.

1. Baking vs. Frying: Pros and Cons

Baking Pros:

Reduced Fat Content: Baked churros have significantly less fat compared to their fried counterparts.

Healthier Option: Baking eliminates the need for submerging churros in oil, making them a more heart-healthy choice.

Ease of Preparation: Baking is less messy and involves less oil handling.

Baking Cons:

Texture Variation: Baked churros may have a slightly different texture, but this can be managed with the right techniques.

Less Intense Flavor: Baking may result in a milder flavor compared to frying, but this can be compensated for with flavorful coatings and fillings.

2. Achieving Crispy Baked Churros

Modified Dough Consistency: Adjust the churro dough by adding a bit more flour to create a slightly thicker consistency, which helps the churros hold their shape during baking.

Preheating the Baking Sheet: Place an empty baking sheet in the oven while it preheats. When ready to bake, transfer the prepared churro dough directly onto the hot baking sheet for an initial burst of heat.

Brushing with Oil: Lightly brush the churros with a small amount of oil before baking. This helps promote browning and contributes to a crispy exterior.

Higher Baking Temperature: Bake the churros at a slightly higher temperature (around 400°F or 200°C) to encourage a quicker browning and a more crisp exterior.

Rotating and Flipping: Rotate the churros and flip them halfway through baking to ensure even browning and crispness on all sides.

Cooling on a Rack: After baking, let the churros cool on a wire rack. This prevents condensation from making them soggy and helps maintain their crispy texture.

3. Flavorful Coatings and Fillings

Cinnamon Sugar Dusting: Roll the warm baked churros in a mixture of cinnamon and sugar to impart a classic and comforting flavor.

Chocolate Drizzle: Drizzle melted chocolate over the baked churros to add a luxurious touch and enhance their sweetness.

Fruit Compote Filling: Fill the baked churros with your favorite fruit compote for a burst of natural sweetness and a satisfying contrast in texture.

Savory Spice Blend: Experiment with savory spice blends as coatings, such as a blend of smoked paprika, garlic powder, and cayenne pepper.

With the techniques of baking versus frying at your fingertips and the knowledge of achieving crispy baked churros, you'll be able to enjoy the delightful crunch and flavor of churros without the guilt. In the upcoming chapters, we'll explore options for those with dietary restrictions, including gluten-free and vegan churro recipes that allow everyone to savor these treats.

Chapter 10: Gluten-Free Churro Options

Celebrate inclusivity with gluten-free churro options that allow everyone to indulge in this beloved treat. In this chapter, we'll dive into the world of gluten-free churros, exploring alternative flour substitutes and sharing valuable tips for handling gluten-free dough. Whether you have dietary restrictions or simply want to enjoy a gluten-free version of churros, you'll discover how to create these treats without compromising on taste or texture.

1. Gluten-Free Flour Substitutes

Rice Flour: A common gluten-free option, rice flour offers a mild flavor and works well in churro recipes.

Almond Flour: Almond flour adds a nutty richness to your churros and contributes to a tender texture.

Chickpea Flour: Chickpea flour adds a unique flavor and a slightly denser texture to your gluten-free churros.

Tapioca Flour/Starch: Tapioca flour helps improve the binding properties of the dough and contributes to a light and crispy exterior.

1:1 Gluten-Free Flour Blends: Pre-made gluten-free flour blends can be a convenient option, offering a combination of different flours to mimic the texture of all-purpose flour.

2. Tips for Gluten-Free Dough Handling

Hydration: Gluten-free flours may require different hydration levels. Adjust the amount of liquid in your recipe to achieve the right dough consistency.

Texture Enhancement: Add xanthan gum or guar gum to your gluten-free flour to improve the dough's elasticity and mimic the stretchiness of gluten.

Resting Time: Allow the gluten-free dough to rest before piping and frying. This gives the flours time to absorb the liquid and results in a more cohesive dough.

Piping Technique: Gluten-free dough may be slightly softer and stickier. Pipe the dough with care, and if needed, dust your hands and piping equipment with additional gluten-free flour to prevent sticking.

Frying Adjustments: Gluten-free churros may brown more quickly than traditional churros. Keep a close eye on them to avoid over-browning.

3. Flavorful Coatings and Variations

Cinnamon Sugar Blend: Roll warm gluten-free churros in a blend of cinnamon and sugar for a classic flavor combination.

Chocolate Ganache: Dip or drizzle your gluten-free churros with velvety chocolate ganache for a decadent touch.

Fruit Compote: Elevate your gluten-free churros with a luscious fruit compote filling, adding a burst of natural sweetness.

Savory Herb Blend: Experiment with a savory blend of herbs and spices for a unique twist on gluten-free churros.

With the knowledge of gluten-free flour substitutes and expert tips for handling gluten-free dough, you'll be able to enjoy the delight of churros without worrying about dietary restrictions.

Chapter 11: Vegan Churro Creations

Embrace a plant-based lifestyle without sacrificing the joy of churro indulgence. In this chapter, we'll venture into the realm of vegan churro creations, exploring alternative ingredients for eggs and dairy and showcasing delicious vegan chocolate and caramel sauces. Whether you're vegan or simply looking to enjoy churros with a cruelty-free twist, you'll discover how to create these delectable treats that are kind to both your taste buds and the planet.

1. Egg and Dairy Replacements

Flaxseed Eggs: Mix ground flaxseed with water to create a flaxseed egg substitute that provides binding and moisture to the dough.

Aquafaba: The liquid from a can of chickpeas, known as aquafaba, is an excellent egg replacement that adds structure and fluffiness to vegan churros.

Plant-Based Milk: Replace dairy milk with your favorite plant-based milk, such as almond, soy, oat, or coconut milk.

Vegan Butter: opt for vegan butter or margarine to achieve the same richness and fat content as traditional butter.

2. Vegan Chocolate and Caramel Sauces
Vegan Chocolate Sauce:

- 1 cup vegan chocolate chips
- ½ cup coconut milk (full fat)
- 1 tablespoon maple syrup (or sweetener of choice)
- Pinch of salt

Vegan Caramel Sauce:

- 1 cup coconut cream (full fat)
- ½ cup coconut sugar
- 2 tablespoons almond butter (or other nut butter)
- 1 teaspoon vanilla extract
- Pinch of salt

Instructions:
Vegan Chocolate Sauce:

1. In a small saucepan, heat the coconut milk until it just begins to simmer.
2. Remove from heat and add vegan chocolate chips, maple syrup, and a pinch of salt.
3. Let sit for a minute, then stir until the chocolate is fully melted and the sauce is smooth.

Vegan Caramel Sauce:

1. In a saucepan, combine coconut cream and coconut sugar. Heat over medium heat until the sugar dissolves.
2. Simmer for about 5-7 minutes, stirring occasionally, until the mixture thickens and turns a caramel color.

3. Remove from heat and stir in almond butter, vanilla extract, and a pinch of salt until smooth.

3. Flavorful Coatings and Variations

Cinnamon Sugar Dusting: Roll warm vegan churros in a mixture of cinnamon and sugar for a classic and comforting flavor.

Vegan Chocolate Drizzle: Drizzle your vegan churros with the homemade vegan chocolate sauce for a decadent touch.

Fruit Compote Filling: Fill your vegan churros with a luscious fruit compote, adding a burst of natural sweetness.

Savory Herb Blend: Experiment with savory herb blends as coatings, such as a blend of rosemary, thyme, and garlic powder.

With the knowledge of egg and dairy replacements and the recipes for vegan chocolate and caramel sauces, you'll be well-equipped to create delectable vegan churro creations that satisfy your cravings and align with your plant-based values.

Chapter 12: Churro-Inspired Breakfast Delights

Start your day with a touch of churro magic by infusing your breakfast favorites with the flavors of these beloved treats. In this chapter, we'll explore churro-inspired breakfast delights that will make your mornings extra special. From churro pancakes and waffles to innovative churro French toast variations, you'll discover how to bring the essence of churros to your breakfast table.

1. Churro Pancakes and Waffles

Churro Pancakes:

- 1 cup all-purpose flour
- 2 tablespoons granulated sugar
- 2 teaspoons baking powder
- ¼ teaspoon salt
- 1 teaspoon ground cinnamon
- ¾ cup plant-based milk
- 1 tablespoon apple cider vinegar
- 1 tablespoon vegetable oil
- 1 teaspoon vanilla extract

Churro Waffles:

- 1 ½ cups all-purpose flour
- 3 tablespoons granulated sugar
- 2 teaspoons baking powder
- ¼ teaspoon salt
- 1 teaspoon ground cinnamon

- 1 ¼ cups plant-based milk
- 1 tablespoon apple cider vinegar
- 3 tablespoons vegetable oil
- 1 teaspoon vanilla extract

Instructions:

1. In separate bowls, whisk together the dry ingredients for either the churro pancakes or churro waffles.
2. In a separate bowl, combine the plant-based milk and apple cider vinegar. Let it sit for a few minutes to curdle, creating a vegan buttermilk.
3. Add the vegetable oil and vanilla extract to the milk mixture and stir to combine.
4. Pour the wet ingredients into the dry ingredients and mix until just combined. Do not overmix; a few lumps are okay.
5. For pancakes: Heat a non-stick skillet or griddle over medium heat. Pour ¼ cup of batter for each pancake and cook until bubbles form on the surface. Flip and cook until golden brown.
6. For waffles: Preheat a waffle iron and lightly grease with oil. Pour enough batter to cover the center of the waffle iron and cook according to the manufacturer's instructions.

2. Churro French Toast Innovations

Churro French Toast Batter:

- 1 cup plant-based milk
- 2 tablespoons chickpea flour (or other egg substitute)
- 2 tablespoons granulated sugar
- 1 teaspoon ground cinnamon
- ½ teaspoon vanilla extract
- Pinch of salt

Instructions:

1. In a bowl, whisk together the plant-based milk, chickpea flour, sugar, ground cinnamon, vanilla extract, and a pinch of salt to create the churro French toast batter.
2. Dip slices of bread into the batter, ensuring both sides are coated.
3. Cook the dipped bread slices on a greased skillet or griddle over medium heat until golden brown on both sides.

Serving Suggestions:

1. Dust the churro pancakes, waffles, or French toast with cinnamon sugar before serving.
2. Drizzle them with homemade chocolate or caramel sauce for an extra touch of decadence.
3. Serve with fresh berries, sliced bananas, or a dollop of coconut whipped cream for a delightful breakfast treat.

With the recipes for churro pancakes, waffles, and innovative churro French toast, your breakfast table will be transformed into a churro-inspired haven, starting your day with warmth and indulgence.

Chapter 13: Churro-Inspired Desserts Beyond Churros

Elevate your dessert game with churro-inspired creations that go beyond the traditional churro. In this chapter, we'll explore delectable churro-inspired desserts that incorporate the beloved flavors and textures of churros into new and exciting treats. From churro ice cream sandwiches to indulgent churro cupcakes and puddings, you'll discover a world of sweet delights that pay homage to the classic churro.

1. Churro Ice Cream Sandwiches
Churro Cookies:

- 1 ½ cups all-purpose flour
- 1 teaspoon baking powder
- ½ teaspoon ground cinnamon
- ¼ teaspoon salt
- ½ cup vegan butter, softened
- ½ cup granulated sugar
- ¼ cup brown sugar
- 2 tablespoons aquafaba (liquid from a can of chickpeas)
- 1 teaspoon vanilla extract

Assembly:

1. Your favorite vegan ice cream
2. Cinnamon sugar for rolling

Instructions:

1. Preheat the oven to 350°F (175°C) and line baking sheets with parchment paper.
2. In a bowl, whisk together the flour, baking powder, ground cinnamon, and salt.
3. In a separate bowl, cream the vegan butter, granulated sugar, and brown sugar until light and fluffy.
4. Add the aquafaba and vanilla extract to the butter mixture and beat until well combined.
5. Gradually add the dry ingredients to the wet ingredients and mix until a dough forms.
6. Roll the dough into small balls and roll each ball in cinnamon sugar.
7. Place the balls on the prepared baking sheets and flatten them slightly with your fingers.
8. Bake for 10-12 minutes, or until the edges are golden brown. Let the cookies cool completely.

Assembly:

1. Take two churro cookies and place a scoop of your favorite vegan ice cream between them.
2. Roll the edges of the ice cream sandwiches in additional cinnamon sugar.
3. Freeze the ice cream sandwiches for at least 1 hour

before serving.

2. Churro Cupcakes and Puddings
Churro Cupcakes:

- 1 ½ cups all-purpose flour
- 1 ½ teaspoons baking powder
- ½ teaspoon ground cinnamon
- ¼ teaspoon salt
- ½ cup vegan butter, softened
- ¾ cup granulated sugar
- 2 tablespoons aquafaba (liquid from a can of chickpeas)
- 1 teaspoon vanilla extract
- ½ cup plant-based milk

Cinnamon Sugar Coating:

- ¼ cup vegan butter, melted
- ½ cup granulated sugar
- 1 teaspoon ground cinnamon

Churro Puddings:

- 2 cups plant-based milk
- ½ cup granulated sugar
- ¼ cup cornstarch
- ½ teaspoon ground cinnamon
- Pinch of salt
- 1 teaspoon vanilla extract

Instructions:
Churro Cupcakes:

1. Preheat the oven to 350°F (175°C) and line a muffin tin with cupcake liners.
2. In a bowl, whisk together the flour, baking powder, ground cinnamon, and salt.
3. In a separate bowl, cream the vegan butter and granulated sugar until light and fluffy.
4. Add the aquafaba and vanilla extract to the butter mixture and beat until well combined.
5. Gradually add the dry ingredients to the wet ingredients, alternating with the plant-based milk, and mix until smooth.
6. Divide the batter evenly among the cupcake liners and bake for 18-20 minutes, or until a toothpick inserted into the center comes out clean.
7. Let the cupcakes cool completely.

Cinnamon Sugar Coating:

1. In a shallow bowl, combine the granulated sugar and ground cinnamon.
2. Dip the cooled cupcakes in melted vegan butter, then roll them in the cinnamon sugar mixture to coat.

Churro Puddings:

1. In a saucepan, whisk together the plant-based milk, granulated sugar, cornstarch, ground cinnamon, and salt.
2. Cook over medium heat, stirring constantly, until the mixture thickens and comes to a gentle boil.
3. Remove from heat and stir in the vanilla extract.

4. Pour the pudding into individual serving dishes and let them cool to room temperature before refrigerating.

Serving Suggestions:

1. Serve the churro ice cream sandwiches, cupcakes, and puddings with a drizzle of vegan chocolate sauce for an extra layer of indulgence.
2. Garnish with a sprinkle of cinnamon sugar or crushed churro cookies.

With these churro-inspired dessert recipes, you'll take the flavors of churros to new heights, creating unforgettable treats that are sure to delight and impress.

Chapter 14: Churro-Inspired Beverages

Quench your thirst and warm your soul with a delightful array of churro-inspired beverages that capture the essence of these beloved treats. In this chapter, we'll explore a range of churro-infused drinks, from comforting churro hot chocolate and coffee blends to indulgent churro milkshakes and energizing churro smoothies. Elevate your beverage game with these creative concoctions that are perfect for sipping and savoring.

1. Churro Hot Chocolate and Coffee Blends
   Churro Hot Chocolate:

- 2 cups plant-based milk
- ¼ cup vegan chocolate chips
- 2 tablespoons cocoa powder
- 2 tablespoons granulated sugar
- 1 teaspoon ground cinnamon
- ½ teaspoon vanilla extract
- Pinch of salt
- Vegan whipped cream and cinnamon sticks for garnish

Churro Coffee Blend:

- Your favorite brewed coffee
- 1 teaspoon ground cinnamon
- ½ teaspoon vanilla extract
- Plant-based milk, frothed (optional)
- Whipped cream and ground cinnamon for garnish

Instructions:
Churro Hot Chocolate:

1. In a saucepan, heat the plant-based milk over medium heat until hot but not boiling.
2. Add vegan chocolate chips, cocoa powder, granulated sugar, ground cinnamon, vanilla extract, and a pinch of salt.
3. Whisk until the chocolate is fully melted and the mixture is smooth.
4. Pour the hot chocolate into mugs and top with vegan whipped cream and a cinnamon stick.

Churro Coffee Blend:

Brew your favorite coffee using your preferred method.

1. In a separate cup, mix ground cinnamon and vanilla extract.
2. Pour the brewed coffee over the cinnamon-vanilla mixture and stir.
3. If desired, froth plant-based milk and add it to the coffee.
4. Top with whipped cream and a sprinkle of ground

cinnamon.

2.   Churro   Milkshakes   and Smoothies

Churro Milkshake:

- 2 cups plant-based vanilla ice cream
- 1 cup plant-based milk
- 2 tablespoons granulated sugar
- 1 teaspoon ground cinnamon
- Vegan whipped cream and cinnamon sugar for garnish

Churro Smoothie:

- 1 banana, frozen
- 1 cup plant-based milk
- 2 tablespoons rolled oats
- 1 tablespoon almond butter (or other nut butter)
- 1 teaspoon ground cinnamon
- ½ teaspoon vanilla extract
- Ice cubes (optional)
- Ground cinnamon for garnish

Instructions:
Churro Milkshake:

1. In a blender, combine plant-based vanilla ice cream, plant-based milk, granulated sugar, and ground cinnamon.
2. Blend until smooth and creamy.
3. Pour the milkshake into glasses and top with vegan

whipped cream and a sprinkle of cinnamon sugar.

Churro Smoothie:

1. In a blender, combine the frozen banana, plant-based milk, rolled oats, almond butter, ground cinnamon, and vanilla extract.
2. Blend until smooth. If desired, add ice cubes for a colder and thicker texture.
3. Pour the smoothie into glasses and garnish with a sprinkle of ground cinnamon.

Serving Suggestions:

1. Serve the churro hot chocolate and coffee blends with a side of churros for dipping.
2. Enjoy the churro milkshakes and smoothies as a refreshing and energizing snack.
3. With these churro-inspired beverage recipes, you'll be able to savor the flavors of churros in a variety of delightful and refreshing drinks.

Chapter 15: DIY Churro Bar: Party Pleasers

Turn any gathering into a churro extravaganza with a DIY Churro Bar that will delight your guests and create unforgettable memories. In this chapter, we'll guide you through setting up a churro toppings bar and interactive churro-making stations, allowing your guests to customize their own churro creations and experience the joy of churro-making together.

1. Setting Up a Churro Toppings Bar
Churro Base:

- Prepare a batch of classic churro dough.

Toppings and Fillings:

- Cinnamon sugar
- Powdered sugar
- Chocolate sauce
- Caramel sauce
- Whipped cream
- Fresh berries
- Sliced bananas
- Chopped nuts (e.g., almonds, pecans)
- Shredded coconut
- Sprinkles

Instructions:

1. Set up a designated area for your churro toppings bar,

ensuring there's ample space for guests to create their own churro masterpieces.

2. Display each topping and filling in individual bowls or jars, making them easily accessible for your guests.

3. Place a tray of warm churros at the center of the toppings bar, ready for guests to start assembling their creations.

4. Provide serving utensils, such as tongs and spoons, for guests to scoop and drizzle their desired toppings.

2. Interactive Churro-Making Stations
Piping and Frying Station:

1. Set up a station where guests can watch and participate in the churro piping and frying process.
2. Provide pre-made churro dough and piping bags filled with dough for guests to try their hand at piping churros onto a baking sheet.
3. Have a frying station nearby, complete with safety precautions and guidelines for guests to fry their own churros.

Coating and Filling Station:

1. Offer a variety of coatings and fillings for guests to choose from, such as cinnamon sugar, chocolate sauce, and fruit compotes.
2. Provide tools for guests to coat their churros, such as shakers for powdered sugar and bowls for dipping sauces.
3. Set out options for filling churros, such as pastry bags filled with chocolate or caramel sauce.

Decor and Ambiance:

1. Create a festive atmosphere with churro-themed decorations, such as banners, signs, and tablecloths in warm and inviting colors.
2. Play fun and upbeat music to set the mood for the churro-making experience.
3. Consider providing aprons or chef's hats for guests to

wear as they participate in the churro-making process.

Guest Activities:

1. Encourage guests to take photos of their churro creations and share them on social media with a designated hashtag.
2. Provide recipe cards with instructions for making churros at home, so guests can recreate the experience after the party.

With a DIY Churro Bar and interactive churro-making stations, your churro-themed party will be a hit, allowing guests to get creative, bond over the joy of churro-making, and enjoy a truly immersive and delicious experience.

Chapter 16: Churro Presentation and Serving Ideas

Elevate the art of churro enjoyment with expert presentation and serving techniques that will leave your guests in awe. In this final chapter, we'll explore plating methods for stunning churro presentations, as well as guide you through pairing churros with wine and cocktails, creating a complete sensory experience that celebrates the delightful world of churros.

1. Plating Techniques for Stunning Presentations

Churro Tower:

Stack churros in a tall and elegant tower, drizzling them with chocolate and caramel sauces for a dramatic effect.

Artful Arrangements:

Arrange churros in a visually appealing pattern, such as a circular design or a swirl, to create a captivating centerpiece.

Churro Bites:

Serve bite-sized churros in decorative cups or shot glasses for a chic and convenient dessert option.

Churro Nest:

Place churros in a nest-like arrangement on a plate, accompanied by colorful berries and a dusting of powdered sugar.

2. Pairing Churros with Wine and Cocktails

Wine Pairings:

Sweet and semi-sweet wines, such as late-harvest Riesling or Moscato, complement the sweetness of churros.

Bold red wines with berry notes, like Zinfandel or Malbec, can provide a delightful contrast to the richness of churros.

Cocktail Companions:

Churro Martini:

Combine vanilla vodka, cinnamon liqueur, and cream liqueur in a shaker with ice. Shake well and strain into a martini glass. Garnish with a cinnamon stick.

Churro Old Fashioned:

Muddle a sugar cube and a few dashes of aromatic bitters in a glass. Add bourbon and ice, then stir. Garnish with an orange twist and a sprinkle of ground cinnamon.

Churro Horchata Cocktail:

Mix equal parts of horchata and spiced rum in a glass filled with ice. Stir gently and garnish with a cinnamon stick.

3. Creative Serving Vessels

Churro Cones:

Create edible churro cones by rolling churros into cone shapes and filling them with ice cream or whipped cream.

Churro Bowls:

Mold warm churros into bowls and fill them with fruit compote, chocolate sauce, or other delectable fillings.

Churro Skewers:

Thread bite-sized churro pieces onto skewers, alternating with fruits like strawberries, bananas, and kiwi.

Churro Sundae:

Layer churro bites, ice cream, sauces, and toppings in a dessert glass to create a delightful churro-inspired sundae.

With these creative presentation and serving ideas, you'll be able to showcase your churros in a way that not only tantalizes the taste buds but also captures the imagination.

Chapter 17: Troubleshooting Churro Mishaps

Even the most experienced churro-makers encounter challenges from time to time. In this chapter, we'll address common churro-making mistakes and provide expert guidance on how to salvage and fix issues, ensuring that your churro creations turn out perfect every time. With these troubleshooting tips at your fingertips, you'll be equipped to handle any churro mishap that comes your way.

1. Common Churro-Making Mistakes

Churros are Too Dense:

Possible Causes: Overmixing the dough, using too much flour, or not letting the dough rest.

Solution: Be gentle when mixing the dough, use the right amount of flour, and allow the dough to rest for the recommended time.

Churros are Soggy or Oily:

Possible Causes: Oil not hot enough, churros left in oil for too long, or excess moisture in the dough.

Solution: Ensure the oil is at the correct temperature, fry churros in small batches, and pat the churros dry before frying.

Churros are Too Pale or Undercooked:

Possible Causes: Oil not hot enough, churros not fried for long enough, or dough too thick.

Solution: Maintain the proper frying temperature, cook churros until golden brown, and ensure the dough is the right consistency.

Churros are Irregularly Shaped:

Possible Causes: Uneven piping or dough consistency, causing churros to break during frying.

Solution: Practice piping consistently sized churros and ensure the dough is well-mixed and smooth.

2. How to Salvage and Fix Issues

Dough is Too Thin:

Solution: Add a bit more flour to the dough to thicken it before piping.

Dough is Too Thick:

Solution: Gradually add a small amount of plant-based milk to the dough until it reaches the desired consistency.

Churros Stick to Piping Bag:

Solution: Lightly grease the inside of the piping bag with oil or cooking spray.

Churros Are Overcooked on the Outside and Raw Inside:

Solution: Lower the frying temperature slightly and ensure the churros are cooked evenly on all sides.

Churros are Not Crispy After Cooling:

Solution: Allow the churros to cool on a wire rack to prevent condensation from making them soggy.

Churros are Too Sweet or Not Sweet Enough:

Solution: Adjust the amount of sugar in the dough and coating to achieve the desired sweetness level.

Churros Lose Their Shape During Frying:

Solution: Pipe churros onto parchment paper and freeze them briefly before frying to help them hold their shape.

With these troubleshooting tips in your arsenal, you'll be able to navigate through any churro-making mishap with confidence. Remember that churro-making is a skill that improves with practice, and even if you encounter challenges, the delicious results are always worth the effort.

Chapter 18: Churro Storage and Reheating

Preserve the deliciousness of your churro creations with expert knowledge on proper storage and reheating techniques. In this chapter, we'll guide you through the best methods for storing your churros and offer tips for reheating them to maintain their fresh, crispy texture and irresistible flavors.

1. Proper Storage Methods

Storing Freshly Made Churros:

1. Allow churros to cool completely before storing.
2. Place churros in an airtight container or resealable plastic bag.
3. Store churros at room temperature for up to 1-2 days for the best texture and flavor.

Freezing Churros:

1. Arrange cooled churros in a single layer on a baking sheet.
2. Place the baking sheet in the freezer until churros are frozen solid.
3. Transfer the frozen churros to a resealable freezer bag or airtight container.
4. Frozen churros can be stored for up to 1-2 months.

2. Reheating Churros for Freshness
Reheating Churros in the Oven:

1. Preheat your oven to 350°F (175°C).
2. Place frozen or room temperature churros on a baking sheet in a single layer.
3. Bake for 5-8 minutes, or until the churros are heated through and crispy.

Reheating Churros in the Microwave:

1. Place a damp paper towel over the churros to prevent them from drying out.
2. Microwave on medium power in 10-15 second intervals until churros are warm.

Reheating Churros in a Skillet:

1. Heat a non-stick skillet over medium heat.
2. Place churros in the skillet and cook for 1-2 minutes on each side until heated and slightly crispy.

Tips for Reheating:

1. Reheating times may vary based on the size and thickness of the churros.
2. If reheating a large quantity of churros, consider using an oven to ensure even reheating.
3. Reheated churros may not be as crisp as freshly fried ones, but these methods will help restore their deliciousness.

3. Churro-Inspired Leftover Treats

Churro French Toast:

Slice day-old churros and use them to make a churro-inspired French toast by dipping them in a mixture of plant-based milk, cinnamon, and vanilla extract before cooking.

Churro Bread Pudding:

Cube leftover churros and use them as a base for a rich and indulgent churro bread pudding.

Churro Crumbs and Toppings:

Crush leftover churros into crumbs and use them as a topping for desserts like ice cream, yogurt, or fruit.

By mastering the art of churro storage and reheating, you'll be able to enjoy the deliciousness of your churro creations long after they're freshly made.

Chapter 19: Crafting Churros as Edible Gifts

Spread joy and culinary delight by gifting handmade churros that are as beautiful as they are delicious. In this chapter, we'll explore the art of crafting churros as edible gifts, complete with expert guidance on packaging, personalizing, and presenting your churro creations for special occasions, holidays, or simply to brighten someone's day.

1. Packaging and Gifting Churros

Churro Gift Bags:

1. Place a small batch of churros in decorative cellophane bags or paper treat bags.
2. Tie the bags with colorful ribbons or twine for an added touch of charm.
3. Attach a handwritten note or a printed recipe card with instructions for reheating and serving.

Churro Gift Boxes:

1. Select elegant gift boxes with compartments to hold churros securely.
2. Line the boxes with tissue paper or parchment paper to prevent sticking.
3. Add a personalized label or sticker to the box, indicating the flavor or variety of churros inside.

Churro Jars:

1. Layer churro bites, toppings, and fillings in small mason jars for a visually appealing gift.
2. Include a wooden spoon for easy scooping and serving.

2. Personalizing Churro Gift Ideas

Custom Flavors:

Experiment with unique churro flavors, such as chai-spiced, matcha, or citrus-infused, and create personalized gift sets.

Churro Kits:

Assemble DIY churro kits with pre-measured dry ingredients and a recipe card, allowing recipients to experience the joy of churro-making at home.

Churro Greeting Cards:

Design custom greeting cards featuring mouthwatering churro illustrations and heartfelt messages.

Themed Gift Sets:

Curate themed churro gift sets, such as a "Movie Night Churros" set with caramel and chocolate dipping sauces, or a "Morning Bliss Churros" set with cinnamon sugar and coffee blend.

3. Presentation and Celebration

Churro Gift Wrapping:

Wrap individual churros in parchment paper or wax paper and secure them with twine or ribbon.

Place the wrapped churros in a decorative box or basket for an elegant presentation.

Special Occasions:

Tailor your churro gifts to suit specific occasions, such as birthdays, holidays, weddings, or anniversaries.

Gift Tags and Labels:

Attach personalized gift tags or labels to each churro package, adding a personal touch and indicating the flavor or theme.

Gift Exchange Ideas:

Organize churro-themed gift exchanges or potluck gatherings where everyone brings their own unique churro creations to share and enjoy.

By crafting churros as edible gifts, you'll not only showcase your culinary prowess but also create memorable and heartfelt presents that are sure to delight recipients and make a lasting impression.

Chapter 20: Churro-Themed Celebrations and Events

Elevate your gatherings and celebrations by infusing them with the enchanting flavors and delights of churros. In this final chapter, we'll guide you through churro party planning tips and show you how to make churros the star of the show at your next event, creating a churro-themed celebration that will leave a lasting impression on your guests.

1. Churro Party Planning Tips
Invitations:

1. Design invitations that feature churro illustrations or graphics, setting the tone for the churro-themed celebration.

Decor and Ambiance:

1. Use warm and inviting colors, such as shades of gold, brown, and cinnamon, to create a cozy and festive atmosphere.
2. Decorate with churro-themed banners, tablecloths, and centerpieces to add a touch of whimsy and delight.

Churro Station:

1. Set up a churro-making station where guests can watch, participate, and customize their own churro creations.
2. Provide a variety of coatings, fillings, and toppings for guests to choose from.

Menu Planning:

Curate a menu that features a range of churro-inspired dishes, from appetizers to desserts, showcasing the versatility of churros.

Themed Activities:

Organize churro-related games or activities, such as a churro decorating contest or a churro trivia game.

2. Churros as a Unique Event Highlight
Churro-Centric Dessert Tables:
Create an eye-catching dessert table filled with a variety of churros, churro-inspired desserts, and decadent toppings.

Churro Wedding Favors:
Offer churros as unique and memorable wedding favors, beautifully packaged for guests to take home.

Churro Bar at Corporate Events:
Surprise attendees at corporate events with a churro bar, providing a delightful and interactive treat during breaks.

Churro-Themed Birthdays:
Craft a churro-themed birthday party with churro-shaped decorations, a churro cake, and churro-inspired activities.

Churro Baby Showers:
Celebrate the impending arrival of a little one with a churro-themed baby shower, featuring adorable churro-themed decorations and treats.

By incorporating churros into your celebrations and events, you'll not only create a unique and unforgettable experience for your guests but also share your passion for the delightful world of churros. Your churro cookbook journey has now come full circle, inspiring you to embrace the joy of churros in every aspect of life's celebrations.

As we conclude this churro cookbook journey, we invite you to savor the memories, flavors, and creativity that you've discovered throughout these pages. From mastering the art of churro-making to exploring a wide array of churro variations, fillings, coatings, and presentations, you've unlocked the secrets to crafting churros that are not only delicious but also a reflection of your culinary artistry.

Churros, with their golden crunchiness and delectable sweetness, have a timeless charm that transcends cultures and generations. Whether enjoyed as a beloved classic or reimagined into innovative creations, churros have the power to bring joy, warmth, and togetherness to any occasion.

From intimate gatherings to grand celebrations, from cozy evenings to festive events, churros have taken center stage and enchanted the palates of all who have tasted their magic. The journey you've embarked upon in this cookbook is more than just a collection of recipes – it's an exploration of creativity, a celebration of flavors, and an invitation to share the delight of churros with those you hold dear.

As you venture forward, we encourage you to continue experimenting, innovating, and crafting your own churro masterpieces. With the knowledge and inspiration gained from this cookbook, may you create churros that not only tantalize the taste buds but also nourish the soul with the simple pleasure of sharing a delicious treat.

Thank you for joining us on this churro adventure. May your churro-making endeavors be filled with joy, satisfaction, and the sheer delight of creating something truly extraordinary.

Happy churro-making, and may your culinary journey be as sweet and satisfying as the churros you create!